My

ROADTRIP

Journal

_____

_____

_____

Date _____ Time _____

Weather Forecast _____
_____

Who with? _____
_____

Departing from: _____ Destination: _____

Odometer Reading _____ $ _____ per gallon _____ gallons

Total Miles: _____ Total Cost: _____

Route Taken _____
_____
_____

Sights/Memorable Events

Pit Stops

☐
☐
☐
☐
☐
☐
☐
☐
☐
☐

Sleepover & Dining Stops

☐
☐
☐
☐
☐
☐
☐
☐
☐
☐

Highlights

_____
_____
_____
_____
_____
_____
_____

Places to Remember for Next Time

_____
_____
_____
_____

Route/Map/Photo/Sketch

Date _____ Time _____

Weather Forecast _____

_____

Who with? _____

_____

Departing from: _____ *Destination:* _____

Odometer Reading _____ $ ____ *per gallon* ____ *gallons*

Total Miles: _____ Total Cost: _____

Route Taken _____

_____

_____

Sights/Memorable Events

Pit Stops   *Sleepover & Dining Stops*

- ☐
- ☐
- ☐
- ☐
- ☐
- ☐
- ☐
- ☐
- ☐
- ☐

Highlights

_____
_____
_____
_____
_____
_____
_____

Places to Remember for Next Time

_____
_____
_____
_____

Route/Map/Photo/Sketch

Date _____ **Time** _____

Weather Forecast _____

Who with? _____

_____

Departing From: _____ *Destination:* _____

Odometer Reading _____ $ _____ *per gallon* _____ *gallons*

Total Miles: _____ Total Cost: _____

Route Taken _____

_____

Sights/Memorable Events

Pit Stops

- ☐
- ☐
- ☐
- ☐
- ☐
- ☐
- ☐
- ☐
- ☐
- ☐

Sleepover & Dining Stops

- ☐
- ☐
- ☐
- ☐
- ☐
- ☐
- ☐
- ☐
- ☐
- ☐

Highlights

_____
_____
_____
_____
_____
_____
_____

Places to Remember for Next Time

_____
_____
_____
_____

Route/Map/Photo/Sketch

Date _____ # Time _____

Weather Forecast _____

_____

Who with? _____

_____

Departing From: _____ *Destination:* _____

Odometer Reading _____ $ ___ *per gallon* ___ *gallons*

Total Miles: _____ # Total Cost: _____

Route Taken _____

_____

_____

Sights/Memorable Events

Pit Stops

- [ ]
- [ ]
- [ ]
- [ ]
- [ ]
- [ ]
- [ ]
- [ ]
- [ ]
- [ ]

Sleepover & Dining Stops

- [ ]
- [ ]
- [ ]
- [ ]
- [ ]
- [ ]
- [ ]
- [ ]
- [ ]
- [ ]

Highlights

_____
_____
_____
_____
_____
_____
_____

Places to Remember for Next Time

_____
_____
_____
_____

Route/Map/Photo/Sketch

Date _____ Time _____
Weather Forecast _____

Who with? _____

Departing from: _____ *Destination:* _____
Odometer Reading _____ $ ___ *per gallon* ___ *gallons*

Total Miles: _____ Total Cost: _____

Route Taken _____

_____

_____

Sights/Memorable Events

Pit Stops

☐
☐
☐
☐
☐
☐
☐
☐
☐
☐

Sleepover & Dining Stops

☐
☐
☐
☐
☐
☐
☐
☐
☐
☐

Highlights

_____
_____
_____
_____
_____
_____
_____

Places to Remember for Next Time

_____
_____
_____
_____
_____

Route/Map/Photo/Sketch

Date _____ Time _____
Weather Forecast _____

Who with? _____
_____

Departing From: _____ *Destination:* _____
Odometer Reading _____ $ ____ *per gallon* ____ *gallons*

Total Miles: _____ Total Cost: _____
Route Taken _____
_____
_____

Sights/Memorable Events

Pit Stops

☐
☐
☐
☐
☐
☐
☐
☐
☐
☐

Sleepover & Dining Stops

☐
☐
☐
☐
☐
☐
☐
☐
☐
☐

Highlights

_____
_____
_____
_____
_____
_____
_____

Places to Remember for Next Time

_____
_____
_____
_____

Route/Map/Photo/Sketch

Date _____ Time _____

Weather Forecast _____

Who with? _____

Departing from: _____ *Destination:* _____

Odometer Reading _____ $ ____ *per gallon* ____ *gallons*

Total Miles: _____ Total Cost: _____

Route Taken _____

_____

Sights/Memorable Events

Pit Stops

☐
☐
☐
☐
☐
☐
☐
☐
☐
☐

Sleepover & Dining Stops

☐
☐
☐
☐
☐
☐
☐
☐
☐
☐

Highlights

_____
_____
_____
_____
_____
_____
_____

Places to Remember for Next Time

_____
_____
_____
_____

Route/Map/Photo/Sketch

Date _____ Time _____
Weather Forecast _____
_____

Who with? _____
_____

Departing From: _____ *Destination:* _____
Odometer Reading _____ $ ____ *per gallon* ____ *gallons*

Total Miles: _____ Total Cost: _____
Route Taken _____
_____

Sights/Memorable Events

Pit Stops
☐
☐
☐
☐
☐
☐
☐
☐
☐
☐

Sleepover & Dining Stops
☐
☐
☐
☐
☐
☐
☐
☐
☐
☐

Highlights

_____
_____
_____
_____
_____
_____
_____

Places to Remember for Next Time

_____
_____
_____
_____

Route/Map/Photo/Sketch

Date _____ # Time _____

Weather Forecast _____

Who with? _____

Departing from: _____ *Destination:* _____
Odometer Reading _____ $ ____ *per gallon* ____ *gallons*

Total Miles: _____ # Total Cost: _____

Route Taken _____

_____

Sights/Memorable Events

Pit Stops	*Sleepover & Dining Stops*
☐	☐
☐	☐
☐	☐
☐	☐
☐	☐
☐	☐
☐	☐
☐	☐
☐	☐
☐	☐

Highlights

_____
_____
_____
_____
_____
_____
_____

Places to Remember for Next Time

_____
_____
_____
_____

Route/Map/Photo/Sketch

Date _____ Time _____
Weather Forecast _____

_____

Who with? _____

_____

Departing from: _____ *Destination:* _____
Odometer Reading _____ $ ____ *per gallon* ____ *gallons*

Total Miles: _____ Total Cost: _____

Route Taken _____

_____

_____

Sights/Memorable Events

Pit Stops

☐
☐
☐
☐
☐
☐
☐
☐
☐
☐

Sleepover & Dining Stops

☐
☐
☐
☐
☐
☐
☐
☐
☐
☐

Highlights

_____
_____
_____
_____
_____
_____
_____

Places to Remember for Next Time

_____
_____
_____
_____

Route/Map/Photo/Sketch

Date _____ Time _____
Weather Forecast _____
_____

Who with? _____
_____

Departing from: _____ Destination: _____
Odometer Reading _____ $ ___ per gallon ___ gallons

Total Miles: _____ Total Cost: _____

Route Taken_____
_____

Sights/Memorable Events

Pit Stops

- ☐
- ☐
- ☐
- ☐
- ☐
- ☐
- ☐
- ☐
- ☐
- ☐

Sleepover & Dining Stops

- ☐
- ☐
- ☐
- ☐
- ☐
- ☐
- ☐
- ☐
- ☐
- ☐

Highlights

_____
_____
_____
_____
_____
_____
_____

Places to Remember for Next Time

_____
_____
_____
_____

Route/Map/Photo/Sketch

Date _____ # Time _____

Weather Forecast _____

Who with? _____

Departing From: _____ *Destination:* _____

Odometer Reading _____ $ ____ *per gallon* ____ *gallons*

Total Miles: _____ # Total Cost: _____

Route Taken _____

_____

Sights/Memorable Events

Pit Stops

- [ ]
- [ ]
- [ ]
- [ ]
- [ ]
- [ ]
- [ ]
- [ ]
- [ ]
- [ ]

Sleepover & Dining Stops

- [ ]
- [ ]
- [ ]
- [ ]
- [ ]
- [ ]
- [ ]
- [ ]
- [ ]
- [ ]

Highlights

_____
_____
_____
_____
_____
_____

Places to Remember for Next Time

_____
_____
_____
_____

Route/Map/Photo/Sketch

Date _____ Time _____
Weather Forecast _____

Who with? _____

Departing From: _____ *Destination:* _____
Odometer Reading _____ $ ___ *per gallon* ___ *gallons*

Total Miles: _____ Total Cost: _____

Route Taken _____
_____
_____

Sights/Memorable Events

Pit Stops

- ☐
- ☐
- ☐
- ☐
- ☐
- ☐
- ☐
- ☐
- ☐
- ☐

Sleepover & Dining Stops

- ☐
- ☐
- ☐
- ☐
- ☐
- ☐
- ☐
- ☐
- ☐
- ☐

Highlights

_____
_____
_____
_____
_____
_____
_____

Places to Remember for Next Time

_____
_____
_____
_____

Route/Map/Photo/Sketch

Date _____ Time _____

Weather Forecast _____

Who with? _____

Departing from: _____ *Destination:* _____
Odometer Reading _____ $ ___ *per gallon* ___ *gallons*

Total Miles: _____ Total Cost: _____

Route Taken _____

_____

Sights/Memorable Events

Pit Stops

☐
☐
☐
☐
☐
☐
☐
☐
☐
☐

Sleepover & Dining Stops

☐
☐
☐
☐
☐
☐
☐
☐
☐
☐

Highlights

_____
_____
_____
_____
_____
_____
_____

Places to Remember for Next Time

_____
_____
_____
_____

Route/Map/Photo/Sketch

Date _____ # Time _____

Weather Forecast _____

Who with? _____

_____

Departing From: _____ *Destination:* _____

Odometer Reading _____ $ ___ *per gallon* ___ *gallons*

Total Miles: _____ # Total Cost: _____

Route Taken _____

_____

_____

Sights/Memorable Events

Pit Stops

☐
☐
☐
☐
☐
☐
☐
☐
☐
☐

Sleepover & Dining Stops

☐
☐
☐
☐
☐
☐
☐
☐
☐
☐

Highlights

_____
_____
_____
_____
_____
_____
_____

Places to Remember for Next Time

_____
_____
_____
_____

Route/Map/Photo/Sketch

Date _____ Time _____
Weather Forecast _____

_____

Who with? _____

_____

Departing from: _____ Destination: _____
Odometer Reading _____ $ ___ per gallon ___ gallons

Total Miles: _____ Total Cost: _____

Route Taken_____

_____

Sights/Memorable Events

Pit Stops

- ☐
- ☐
- ☐
- ☐
- ☐
- ☐
- ☐
- ☐
- ☐

Sleepover & Dining Stops

- ☐
- ☐
- ☐
- ☐
- ☐
- ☐
- ☐
- ☐
- ☐

Highlights

_____
_____
_____
_____
_____
_____
_____

Places to Remember for Next Time

_____
_____
_____
_____

Route/Map/Photo/Sketch

Date _____ Time _____

Weather Forecast _____

Who with? _____

Departing from: _____ *Destination:* _____

Odometer Reading _____ $ ___ *per gallon* ___ *gallons*

Total Miles: _____ Total Cost: _____

Route Taken _____

_____

_____

Sights/Memorable Events

Pit Stops

☐
☐
☐
☐
☐
☐
☐
☐
☐
☐

Sleepover & Dining Stops

☐
☐
☐
☐
☐
☐
☐
☐
☐
☐

Highlights

_____
_____
_____
_____
_____
_____
_____

Places to Remember for Next Time

_____
_____
_____
_____

Route/Map/Photo/Sketch

Date _____ # Time _____

Weather Forecast _____

Who with? _____

_____

Departing from: _____   *Destination:* _____

Odometer Reading _____ $ ___ *per gallon* ___ *gallons*

Total Miles: _____ # Total Cost: _____

Route Taken _____

_____

_____

Sights/Memorable Events

Pit Stops

- ☐
- ☐
- ☐
- ☐
- ☐
- ☐
- ☐
- ☐
- ☐
- ☐

Sleepover & Dining Stops

- ☐
- ☐
- ☐
- ☐
- ☐
- ☐
- ☐
- ☐
- ☐
- ☐

Highlights

_____
_____
_____
_____
_____
_____
_____

Places to Remember for Next Time

_____
_____
_____
_____

Route/Map/Photo/Sketch

Date _____ Time _____
Weather Forecast _____

Who with? _____

Departing from: _____ Destination: _____
Odometer Reading _____ $ ____ per gallon ____ gallons

Total Miles: _____ Total Cost: _____

Route Taken_____
_____
_____

Sights/Memorable Events

Pit Stops

☐
☐
☐
☐
☐
☐
☐
☐
☐
☐

Sleepover & Dining Stops

☐
☐
☐
☐
☐
☐
☐
☐
☐
☐

Highlights

_____
_____
_____
_____
_____
_____

Places to Remember for Next Time

_____
_____
_____
_____

Route/Map/Photo/Sketch

Date _____ Time _____

Weather Forecast _____

Who with? _____

Departing from: _____ *Destination:* _____

Odometer Reading _____ $ ___ *per gallon* ___ *gallons*

Total Miles: _____ Total Cost: _____

Route Taken _____

_____

Sights/Memorable Events

Pit Stops

- [ ]
- [ ]
- [ ]
- [ ]
- [ ]
- [ ]
- [ ]
- [ ]
- [ ]
- [ ]

Sleepover & Dining Stops

- [ ]
- [ ]
- [ ]
- [ ]
- [ ]
- [ ]
- [ ]
- [ ]
- [ ]
- [ ]

Highlights

Places to Remember for Next Time

Route/Map/Photo/Sketch

Date _____ # Time _____

Weather Forecast _____

Who with? _____

Departing from: _____ *Destination:* _____
Odometer Reading _____ $ ____ *per gallon* ____ *gallons*

Total Miles: _____ ## Total Cost: _____

Route Taken _____
_____
_____

Sights/Memorable Events

Pit Stops

☐
☐
☐
☐
☐
☐
☐
☐
☐
☐

Sleepover & Dining Stops

☐
☐
☐
☐
☐
☐
☐
☐
☐
☐

Highlights

_____
_____
_____
_____
_____
_____
_____

Places to Remember for Next Time

_____
_____
_____
_____

Route/Map/Photo/Sketch

Date _____ Time _____

Weather Forecast _____

_____

Who with? _____

_____

Departing From: _____ *Destination:* _____

Odometer Reading _____ $ ___ *per gallon* ___ *gallons*

Total Miles: _____ Total Cost: _____

Route Taken _____

_____

_____

Sights/Memorable Events

Pit Stops

- [ ]
- [ ]
- [ ]
- [ ]
- [ ]
- [ ]
- [ ]
- [ ]
- [ ]
- [ ]

Sleepover & Dining Stops

- [ ]
- [ ]
- [ ]
- [ ]
- [ ]
- [ ]
- [ ]
- [ ]
- [ ]
- [ ]

Highlights

_____
_____
_____
_____
_____
_____
_____

Places to Remember for Next Time

_____
_____
_____
_____

Route/Map/Photo/Sketch

Date _____ Time _____

Weather Forecast _____

_____

Who with? _____

_____

Departing from: _____ *Destination:* _____

Odometer Reading _____ $ ____ *per gallon* ____ *gallons*

Total Miles: _____ Total Cost: _____

Route Taken _____

_____

_____

Sights/Memorable Events

Pit Stops

☐
☐
☐
☐
☐
☐
☐
☐
☐
☐

Sleepover & Dining Stops

☐
☐
☐
☐
☐
☐
☐
☐
☐
☐

Highlights

_____
_____
_____
_____
_____
_____
_____

Places to Remember for Next Time

_____
_____
_____
_____

Route/Map/Photo/Sketch

Date _____ Time _____

Weather Forecast _____

_____

Who with? _____

_____

Departing From: _____ *Destination:* _____

Odometer Reading _____ $ ___ *per gallon* ___ *gallons*

Total Miles: _____ Total Cost: _____

Route Taken _____

_____

_____

Sights/Memorable Events

Pit Stops

☐
☐
☐
☐
☐
☐
☐
☐
☐
☐

Sleepover & Dining Stops

☐
☐
☐
☐
☐
☐
☐
☐
☐
☐

Highlights

_____
_____
_____
_____
_____
_____
_____

Places to Remember for Next Time

_____
_____
_____
_____

Route/Map/Photo/Sketch

Date _____ **Time** _____
Weather Forecast _____

Who with? _____

Departing from: _____ *Destination:* _____
Odometer Reading _____ $ ___ *per gallon* ___ *gallons*

Total Miles: _____ Total Cost: _____
Route Taken _____
_____
_____

Sights/Memorable Events

Pit Stops

- [ ]
- [ ]
- [ ]
- [ ]
- [ ]
- [ ]
- [ ]
- [ ]
- [ ]
- [ ]

Sleepover & Dining Stops

- [ ]
- [ ]
- [ ]
- [ ]
- [ ]
- [ ]
- [ ]
- [ ]
- [ ]
- [ ]

Highlights

_____
_____
_____
_____
_____
_____
_____

Places to Remember for Next Time

_____
_____
_____
_____

Route/Map/Photo/Sketch

Date _____ Time _____

Weather Forecast _____

_____

Who with? _____

_____

Departing From: _____ Destination: _____
Odometer Reading _____ $ ___ per gallon ___ gallons

Total Miles: _____ Total Cost: _____

Route Taken _____

_____

_____

Sights/Memorable Events

Pit Stops

- ☐
- ☐
- ☐
- ☐
- ☐
- ☐
- ☐
- ☐
- ☐
- ☐

Sleepover & Dining Stops

- ☐
- ☐
- ☐
- ☐
- ☐
- ☐
- ☐
- ☐
- ☐
- ☐

Highlights

_____
_____
_____
_____
_____
_____
_____

Places to Remember for Next Time

_____
_____
_____
_____

Route/Map/Photo/Sketch

Date _____ Time _____
Weather Forecast _____

Who with? _____

Departing From: _____ *Destination:* _____
Odometer Reading _____ $ _____ *per gallon* _____ *gallons*

Total Miles: _____ Total Cost: _____

Route Taken _____
_____
_____

Sights/Memorable Events

Pit Stops

☐
☐
☐
☐
☐
☐
☐
☐
☐
☐

Sleepover & Dining Stops

☐
☐
☐
☐
☐
☐
☐
☐
☐
☐

Highlights

_____
_____
_____
_____
_____
_____
_____

Places to Remember for Next Time

_____
_____
_____
_____

Route/Map/Photo/Sketch

Date _____ **Time** _____

Weather Forecast _____

Who with? _____

_____

Departing from: _____ *Destination:* _____

Odometer Reading _____ $ ____ *per gallon* ____ *gallons*

Total Miles: _____ Total Cost: _____

Route Taken _____

_____

_____

Sights/Memorable Events

Pit Stops

☐
☐
☐
☐
☐
☐
☐
☐
☐
☐

Sleepover & Dining Stops

☐
☐
☐
☐
☐
☐
☐
☐
☐
☐

Highlights

_____
_____
_____
_____
_____
_____

Places to Remember for Next Time

_____
_____
_____
_____

Route/Map/Photo/Sketch

Date _____ Time _____

Weather Forecast _____

Who with? _____

_____

Departing From: _____ *Destination:* _____
Odometer Reading _____ $ ___ *per gallon* ___ *gallons*

Total Miles: _____ Total Cost: _____

Route Taken _____

_____

_____

Sights/Memorable Events

Pit Stops

☐
☐
☐
☐
☐
☐
☐
☐
☐
☐

Sleepover & Dining Stops

☐
☐
☐
☐
☐
☐
☐
☐
☐
☐

Highlights

_____
_____
_____
_____
_____
_____

Places to Remember for Next Time

_____
_____
_____
_____

Route/Map/Photo/Sketch

Date _____ **Time** _____

Weather Forecast _____

Who with? _____

Departing From: _____ *Destination:* _____

Odometer Reading _____ $ ___ *per gallon* ___ *gallons*

Total Miles: _____ Total Cost: _____

Route Taken _____
_____
_____

Sights/Memorable Events

Pit Stops

☐
☐
☐
☐
☐
☐
☐
☐
☐
☐

Sleepover & Dining Stops

☐
☐
☐
☐
☐
☐
☐
☐
☐
☐

Highlights

_____
_____
_____
_____
_____
_____
_____

Places to Remember for Next Time

_____
_____
_____
_____

Route/Map/Photo/Sketch

Date _____ Time _____

Weather forecast _____

Who with? _____

Departing from: _____ *Destination:* _____
Odometer Reading _____ $ ____ *per gallon* ____ *gallons*

Total Miles: _____ Total Cost: _____

Route Taken _____

_____

Sights/Memorable Events

Pit Stops

☐
☐
☐
☐
☐
☐
☐
☐
☐
☐

Sleepover & Dining Stops

☐
☐
☐
☐
☐
☐
☐
☐
☐
☐

Highlights

_____
_____
_____
_____
_____
_____
_____

Places to Remember for Next Time

_____
_____
_____
_____

Route/Map/Photo/Sketch

Date _____ Time _____

Weather Forecast _____

_____

Who with? _____

_____

Departing from: _____ *Destination:* _____

Odometer Reading _____ $ ____ *per gallon* ____ *gallons*

Total Miles: _____ Total Cost: _____

Route Taken _____

_____

_____

Sights/Memorable Events

Pit Stops

- [ ]
- [ ]
- [ ]
- [ ]
- [ ]
- [ ]
- [ ]
- [ ]
- [ ]
- [ ]

Sleepover & Dining Stops

- [ ]
- [ ]
- [ ]
- [ ]
- [ ]
- [ ]
- [ ]
- [ ]
- [ ]
- [ ]

Highlights

_____
_____
_____
_____
_____
_____
_____

Places to Remember for Next Time

_____
_____
_____
_____
_____

Route/Map/Photo/Sketch

Date _____ # Time _____

Weather Forecast _____

Who with? _____
_____

Departing from: _____ *Destination:* _____
Odometer Reading _____ $ ___ *per gallon* ___ *gallons*

Total Miles: _____ # Total Cost: _____

Route Taken _____
_____
_____

Sights/Memorable Events

Pit Stops

☐
☐
☐
☐
☐
☐
☐
☐
☐

Sleepover & Dining Stops

☐
☐
☐
☐
☐
☐
☐
☐
☐

Highlights

_____
_____
_____
_____
_____
_____
_____

Places to Remember for Next Time

_____
_____
_____
_____

Route/Map/Photo/Sketch

Date _____ Time _____

Weather Forecast _____

Who with? _____

Departing from: _____ *Destination:* _____

Odometer Reading _____ $ ____ *per gallon* ____ *gallons*

Total Miles: _____ Total Cost: _____

Route Taken _____

_____

_____

Sights/Memorable Events

Pit Stops

☐
☐
☐
☐
☐
☐
☐
☐
☐
☐

Sleepover & Dining Stops

☐
☐
☐
☐
☐
☐
☐
☐
☐
☐

Highlights

_____

_____

_____

_____

_____

_____

Places to Remember for Next Time

_____

_____

_____

_____

Route/Map/Photo/Sketch

Date _____ Time _____
Weather Forecast _____

Who with? _____
_____

Departing from: _____ *Destination:* _____
Odometer Reading _____ $ ____ *per gallon* ____ *gallons*

Total Miles: _____ Total Cost: _____
Route Taken _____
_____
_____

Sights/Memorable Events

Pit Stops

☐
☐
☐
☐
☐
☐
☐
☐
☐
☐

Sleepover & Dining Stops

☐
☐
☐
☐
☐
☐
☐
☐
☐
☐

Highlights

_____

_____

_____

_____

_____

_____

Places to Remember for Next Time

_____

_____

_____

_____

Route/Map/Photo/Sketch

Date _____ Time _____

Weather Forecast _____

_____

Who with? _____

_____

Departing from: _____ *Destination:* _____

Odometer Reading _____ $ ____ *per gallon* ____ *gallons*

Total Miles: _____ Total Cost: _____

Route Taken _____

_____

_____

Sights/Memorable Events

Pit Stops

☐
☐
☐
☐
☐
☐
☐
☐
☐
☐

Sleepover & Dining Stops

☐
☐
☐
☐
☐
☐
☐
☐
☐
☐

Highlights

_____
_____
_____
_____
_____
_____
_____

Places to Remember for Next Time

_____
_____
_____
_____

Route/Map/Photo/Sketch

Date _____ Time _____

Weather Forecast _____

_____

Who with? _____

_____

Departing from: _____ *Destination:* _____
Odometer Reading _____ $ _____ *per gallon* _____ *gallons*

Total Miles: _____ Total Cost: _____

Route Taken _____

_____

Sights/Memorable Events

Pit Stops

- ☐
- ☐
- ☐
- ☐
- ☐
- ☐
- ☐
- ☐
- ☐
- ☐

Sleepover & Dining Stops

- ☐
- ☐
- ☐
- ☐
- ☐
- ☐
- ☐
- ☐
- ☐
- ☐

Highlights

_____
_____
_____
_____
_____
_____
_____

Places to Remember for Next Time

_____
_____
_____
_____

Route/Map/Photo/Sketch

Date _____ Time _____
Weather Forecast _____

_____

Who with? _____

_____

Departing from: _____ *Destination:* _____

Odometer Reading _____ $ ____ *per gallon* ____ *gallons*

Total Miles: _____ Total Cost: _____

Route Taken _____

_____

_____

Sights/Memorable Events

Pit Stops
- ☐
- ☐
- ☐
- ☐
- ☐
- ☐
- ☐
- ☐
- ☐
- ☐

Sleepover & Dining Stops
- ☐
- ☐
- ☐
- ☐
- ☐
- ☐
- ☐
- ☐
- ☐
- ☐

Highlights

_____

_____

_____

_____

_____

_____

_____

Places to Remember for Next Time

_____

_____

_____

_____

Route/Map/Photo/Sketch

Date _____ Time _____

Weather Forecast _____

_____

Who with? _____

_____

Departing from: _____ Destination: _____

Odometer Reading _____ $ ___ per gallon ___ gallons

Total Miles: _____ Total Cost: _____

Route Taken _____

_____

Sights/Memorable Events

Pit Stops

- ☐
- ☐
- ☐
- ☐
- ☐
- ☐
- ☐
- ☐
- ☐
- ☐

Sleepover & Dining Stops

- ☐
- ☐
- ☐
- ☐
- ☐
- ☐
- ☐
- ☐
- ☐
- ☐

Highlights

_____
_____
_____
_____
_____
_____
_____

Places to Remember for Next Time

_____
_____
_____
_____

Route/Map/Photo/Sketch

Date _____ Time _____

Weather Forecast _____

Who with? _____

Departing from: _____ *Destination:* _____
Odometer Reading _____ $ ____ *per gallon* ____ *gallons*

Total Miles:_____ Total Cost: _____

*Route Taken*_____
_____

Sights/Memorable Events

Pit Stops

☐
☐
☐
☐
☐
☐
☐
☐
☐
☐

Sleepover & Dining Stops

☐
☐
☐
☐
☐
☐
☐
☐
☐
☐

Highlights

_____

_____

_____

_____

_____

_____

_____

Places to Remember for Next Time

_____

_____

_____

_____

Route/Map/Photo/Sketch

Date _____ Time _____
Weather Forecast _____

Who with? _____

Departing from: _____ Destination: _____
Odometer Reading _____ $ ____ per gallon ____ gallons

Total Miles: _____ Total Cost: _____
Route Taken _____
_____

Sights/Memorable Events

Pit Stops

☐
☐
☐
☐
☐
☐
☐
☐
☐
☐

Sleepover & Dining Stops

☐
☐
☐
☐
☐
☐
☐
☐
☐
☐

Highlights

Places to Remember for Next Time

Route/Map/Photo/Sketch

Date _____ Time _____

Weather Forecast _____

Who with? _____

_____

Departing from: _____ *Destination:* _____

Odometer Reading _____ $ ___ *per gallon* ___ *gallons*

Total Miles: _____ Total Cost: _____

Route Taken _____

_____

Sights/Memorable Events

Pit Stops

- [ ]
- [ ]
- [ ]
- [ ]
- [ ]
- [ ]
- [ ]
- [ ]
- [ ]
- [ ]

Sleepover & Dining Stops

- [ ]
- [ ]
- [ ]
- [ ]
- [ ]
- [ ]
- [ ]
- [ ]
- [ ]
- [ ]

Highlights

_____
_____
_____
_____
_____
_____
_____

Places to Remember for Next Time

_____
_____
_____
_____

Route/Map/Photo/Sketch

Date _____ Time _____

Weather forecast _____

Who with? _____

_____

Departing from: _____ *Destination:* _____

Odometer Reading _____ $ _____ *per gallon* _____ *gallons*

Total Miles: _____ Total Cost: _____

Route Taken _____

_____

_____

Sights/Memorable Events

Pit Stops

☐
☐
☐
☐
☐
☐
☐
☐
☐
☐

Sleepover & Dining Stops

☐
☐
☐
☐
☐
☐
☐
☐
☐

Highlights

_____
_____
_____
_____
_____
_____
_____

Places to Remember for Next Time

_____
_____
_____
_____

Route/Map/Photo/Sketch

Date _____ # Time _____

Weather Forecast _____

Who with? _____

Departing from: _____ *Destination:* _____

Odometer Reading _____ $ ____ *per gallon* ____ *gallons*

Total Miles: _____ # Total Cost: _____

Route Taken _____

_____

Sights/Memorable Events

Pit Stops

☐
☐
☐
☐
☐
☐
☐
☐
☐
☐

Sleepover & Dining Stops

☐
☐
☐
☐
☐
☐
☐
☐
☐
☐

Highlights

_____
_____
_____
_____
_____
_____
_____
_____

Places to Remember for Next Time

_____
_____
_____
_____

Route/Map/Photo/Sketch

Date _____ Time _____

Weather Forecast _____

Who with? _____

Departing From: _____ *Destination:* _____

Odometer Reading _____ $ ____ *per gallon* ____ *gallons*

Total Miles: _____ Total Cost: _____

Route Taken _____

_____

_____

Sights/Memorable Events

Pit Stops

- [ ]
- [ ]
- [ ]
- [ ]
- [ ]
- [ ]
- [ ]
- [ ]
- [ ]
- [ ]

Sleepover & Dining Stops

- [ ]
- [ ]
- [ ]
- [ ]
- [ ]
- [ ]
- [ ]
- [ ]
- [ ]
- [ ]

Highlights

_____
_____
_____
_____
_____
_____
_____

Places to Remember for Next Time

_____
_____
_____
_____
_____

Route/Map/Photo/Sketch

Date _____ Time _____

Weather Forecast _____

_____

Who with? _____

_____

Departing from: _____ *Destination:* _____

Odometer Reading _____ $ ___ *per gallon* ___ *gallons*

Total Miles: _____ Total Cost: _____

Route Taken _____

_____

_____

Sights/Memorable Events

Pit Stops

- ☐
- ☐
- ☐
- ☐
- ☐
- ☐
- ☐
- ☐
- ☐
- ☐

Sleepover & Dining Stops

- ☐
- ☐
- ☐
- ☐
- ☐
- ☐
- ☐
- ☐
- ☐
- ☐

Highlights

_____
_____
_____
_____
_____
_____
_____

Places to Remember for Next Time

_____
_____
_____
_____

Route/Map/Photo/Sketch

Date _____ Time _____

Weather Forecast _____

Who with? _____

Departing from: _____ **Destination:** _____

Odometer Reading _____ $ ____ per gallon ____ gallons

Total Miles: _____ Total Cost: _____

Route Taken _____

_____

Sights/Memorable Events

_____

_____

_____

_____

_____

Pit Stops

☐
☐
☐
☐
☐
☐
☐
☐
☐
☐

Sleepover & Dining Stops

☐
☐
☐
☐
☐
☐
☐
☐
☐
☐

Highlights

_____

_____

_____

_____

_____

_____

_____

Places to Remember for Next Time

_____

_____

_____

_____

_____

Route/Map/Photo/Sketch

Date _____ Time _____

Weather Forecast _____

Who with? _____

Departing from: _____ *Destination:* _____

Odometer Reading _____ $ ____ *per gallon* ____ *gallons*

Total Miles: _____ Total Cost: _____

Route Taken _____

_____

Sights/Memorable Events

Pit Stops

☐
☐
☐
☐
☐
☐
☐
☐
☐
☐

Sleepover & Dining Stops

☐
☐
☐
☐
☐
☐
☐
☐
☐
☐

Highlights

_____
_____
_____
_____
_____
_____
_____

Places to Remember for Next Time

_____
_____
_____
_____

Route/Map/Photo/Sketch

Date _____ Time _____

Weather Forecast _____

_____

Who with? _____

_____

Departing from: _____ *Destination:* _____

Odometer Reading _____ $ ____ *per gallon* ____ *gallons*

Total Miles: _____ Total Cost: _____

Route Taken _____

_____

Sights/Memorable Events

Pit Stops

- ☐
- ☐
- ☐
- ☐
- ☐
- ☐
- ☐
- ☐
- ☐
- ☐

Sleepover & Dining Stops

- ☐
- ☐
- ☐
- ☐
- ☐
- ☐
- ☐
- ☐
- ☐
- ☐

Highlights

_____

_____

_____

_____

_____

_____

_____

Places to Remember for Next Time

_____

_____

_____

_____

_____

Route/Map/Photo/Sketch

Date _____ Time _____

Weather Forecast _____

_____

Who with? _____

_____

Departing From: _____ Destination: _____

Odometer Reading _____ $ _____ per gallon _____ gallons

Total Miles: _____ Total Cost: _____

Route Taken _____

_____

_____

Sights/Memorable Events

Pit Stops

- ☐
- ☐
- ☐
- ☐
- ☐
- ☐
- ☐
- ☐
- ☐
- ☐

Sleepover & Dining Stops

- ☐
- ☐
- ☐
- ☐
- ☐
- ☐
- ☐
- ☐
- ☐
- ☐

Highlights

_____
_____
_____
_____
_____
_____
_____

Places to Remember for Next Time

_____
_____
_____
_____

Route/Map/Photo/Sketch

Date _____ Time _____

Weather Forecast _____

_____

Who with? _____

_____

Departing from: _____ *Destination:* _____

Odometer Reading _____ $ ___ *per gallon* ___ *gallons*

Total Miles: _____ Total Cost: _____

Route Taken _____

_____

_____

Sights/Memorable Events

Pit Stops

- [ ]
- [ ]
- [ ]
- [ ]
- [ ]
- [ ]
- [ ]
- [ ]
- [ ]
- [ ]

Sleepover & Dining Stops

- [ ]
- [ ]
- [ ]
- [ ]
- [ ]
- [ ]
- [ ]
- [ ]
- [ ]
- [ ]

Highlights

_____
_____
_____
_____
_____
_____
_____

Places to Remember for Next Time

_____
_____
_____
_____

Route/Map/Photo/Sketch

Date _____ Time _____

Weather Forecast _____

Who with? _____

Departing From: _____ Destination: _____

Odometer Reading _____ $ _____ per gallon _____ gallons

Total Miles: _____ Total Cost: _____

Route Taken _____

_____

_____

Sights/Memorable Events

Pit Stops

☐
☐
☐
☐
☐
☐
☐
☐
☐
☐

Sleepover & Dining Stops

☐
☐
☐
☐
☐
☐
☐
☐
☐
☐

Highlights

_____

_____

_____

_____

_____

_____

_____

Places to Remember for Next Time

_____

_____

_____

_____

Route/Map/Photo/Sketch

Date _____ Time _____

Weather Forecast _____

Who with? _____

Departing From: _____ *Destination:* _____

Odometer Reading _____ $ ___ *per gallon* ___ *gallons*

Total Miles: _____ Total Cost: _____

Route Taken _____

_____

_____

Sights/Memorable Events

Pit Stops

- [ ]
- [ ]
- [ ]
- [ ]
- [ ]
- [ ]
- [ ]
- [ ]
- [ ]
- [ ]

Sleepover & Dining Stops

- [ ]
- [ ]
- [ ]
- [ ]
- [ ]
- [ ]
- [ ]
- [ ]
- [ ]
- [ ]

Highlights

Places to Remember for Next Time

Route/Map/Photo/Sketch

Date _____ Time _____

Weather Forecast _____

_____

Who with? _____

_____

Departing from: _____ *Destination:* _____

Odometer Reading _____ $ ____ *per gallon* ____ *gallons*

Total Miles: _____ Total Cost: _____

Route Taken _____

_____

_____

Sights/Memorable Events

Pit Stops

☐
☐
☐
☐
☐
☐
☐
☐
☐
☐

Sleepover & Dining Stops

☐
☐
☐
☐
☐
☐
☐
☐
☐
☐

Highlights

_____
_____
_____
_____
_____
_____
_____

Places to Remember for Next Time

_____
_____
_____
_____

Route / Map / Photo / Sketch

Date _____ Time _____

Weather Forecast _____

_____

Who with? _____

_____

Departing from: _____ *Destination:* _____

Odometer Reading _____ $ ____ *per gallon* ____ *gallons*

Total Miles: _____ Total Cost: _____

Route Taken _____

_____

Sights/Memorable Events

Pit Stops

☐
☐
☐
☐
☐
☐
☐
☐
☐
☐

Sleepover & Dining Stops

☐
☐
☐
☐
☐
☐
☐
☐
☐
☐

Highlights

_____
_____
_____
_____
_____
_____

Places to Remember for Next Time

_____
_____
_____
_____

Route/Map/Photo/Sketch

Date _____ Time _____

Weather Forecast _____

_____

Who with? _____

_____

Departing from: _____ Destination: _____

Odometer Reading _____ $ ____ per gallon ____ gallons

Total Miles: _____ Total Cost: _____

Route Taken_____

_____

Sights/Memorable Events

Pit Stops
- ☐
- ☐
- ☐
- ☐
- ☐
- ☐
- ☐
- ☐
- ☐
- ☐

Sleepover & Dining Stops
- ☐
- ☐
- ☐
- ☐
- ☐
- ☐
- ☐
- ☐
- ☐
- ☐

Highlights

_____
_____
_____
_____
_____
_____
_____

Places to Remember for Next Time

_____
_____
_____
_____

Route/Map/Photo/Sketch

Date _____ Time _____
Weather Forecast _____

Who with? _____

_____

Departing from: _____ Destination: _____

Odometer Reading _____ $ ___ per gallon ___ gallons

Total Miles: _____ Total Cost: _____

Route Taken _____

_____

Sights/Memorable Events

Pit Stops

- ☐
- ☐
- ☐
- ☐
- ☐
- ☐
- ☐
- ☐
- ☐
- ☐

Sleepover & Dining Stops

- ☐
- ☐
- ☐
- ☐
- ☐
- ☐
- ☐
- ☐
- ☐
- ☐

Highlights

_____
_____
_____
_____
_____
_____
_____
_____

Places to Remember for Next Time

_____
_____
_____
_____
_____

Route/Map/Photo/Sketch

Date _____ Time _____

Weather Forecast _____

Who with? _____

_____

Departing from: _____ Destination: _____
Odometer Reading _____ $ ___ per gallon ___ gallons

Total Miles: _____ Total Cost: _____

Route Taken_____

_____

_____

Sights/Memorable Events

Pit Stops

- ☐
- ☐
- ☐
- ☐
- ☐
- ☐
- ☐
- ☐
- ☐
- ☐

Sleepover & Dining Stops

- ☐
- ☐
- ☐
- ☐
- ☐
- ☐
- ☐
- ☐
- ☐
- ☐

Highlights

_____
_____
_____
_____
_____
_____

Places to Remember for Next Time

_____
_____
_____
_____

Route/Map/Photo/Sketch

Date _____ Time _____
Weather Forecast _____

_____

Who with? _____

_____

Departing from: _____ *Destination:* _____

Odometer Reading _____ $ ____ *per gallon* ____ *gallons*

Total Miles: _____ Total Cost: _____

Route Taken _____

_____

_____

Sights/Memorable Events

Pit Stops

- ☐
- ☐
- ☐
- ☐
- ☐
- ☐
- ☐
- ☐
- ☐
- ☐

Sleepover & Dining Stops

- ☐
- ☐
- ☐
- ☐
- ☐
- ☐
- ☐
- ☐
- ☐
- ☐

Highlights

_____
_____
_____
_____
_____
_____
_____

Places to Remember for Next Time

_____
_____
_____
_____
_____

Route/Map/Photo/Sketch

Date _____ Time _____

Weather Forecast _____

_____

Who with? _____

_____

Departing from: _____ *Destination:* _____

Odometer Reading _____ $ _____ *per gallon* _____ *gallons*

Total Miles: _____ Total Cost: _____

Route Taken _____

_____

Sights/Memorable Events

Pit Stops

- ☐
- ☐
- ☐
- ☐
- ☐
- ☐
- ☐
- ☐
- ☐
- ☐

Sleepover & Dining Stops

- ☐
- ☐
- ☐
- ☐
- ☐
- ☐
- ☐
- ☐
- ☐
- ☐

Highlights

_____
_____
_____
_____
_____
_____
_____

Places to Remember for Next Time

_____
_____
_____
_____
_____

Route/Map/Photo/Sketch

Date _____ Time _____

Weather Forecast _____

_____

Who with? _____

_____

Departing from: _____ Destination: _____

Odometer Reading _____ $ _____ per gallon _____ gallons

Total Miles: _____ Total Cost: _____

Route Taken _____

_____

Sights/Memorable Events

Pit Stops

☐
☐
☐
☐
☐
☐
☐
☐
☐
☐

Sleepover & Dining Stops

☐
☐
☐
☐
☐
☐
☐
☐
☐
☐

Highlights

_____
_____
_____
_____
_____
_____

Places to Remember for Next Time

_____
_____
_____
_____

Route/Map/Photo/Sketch

Date _____ Time _____

Weather Forecast _____
_____

Who with? _____
_____

Departing from: _____ Destination: _____
Odometer Reading _____ $ ____ per gallon ____ gallons

Total Miles: _____ Total Cost: _____

Route Taken _____
_____

Sights/Memorable Events

Pit Stops

- [ ]
- [ ]
- [ ]
- [ ]
- [ ]
- [ ]
- [ ]
- [ ]
- [ ]
- [ ]

Sleepover & Dining Stops

- [ ]
- [ ]
- [ ]
- [ ]
- [ ]
- [ ]
- [ ]
- [ ]
- [ ]

Highlights

_____
_____
_____
_____
_____
_____
_____

Places to Remember for Next Time

_____
_____
_____
_____

Route/Map/Photo/Sketch

Manufactured by Amazon.ca
Bolton, ON

19865130R00070